CONTENTS

BRUCE WAYNE
TO THE MANOR BORN

VITAL STATS

LIKES: Bats
DISLIKES: Bats (Bruce is a complex guy!)
FRIENDS: Alfred
FOES: Anyone who might discover his secret identity
SKILLS: Brilliant businessman
GEAR: Secret hideout

SET NAMES: The Batcave: The Penguin and Mr. Freeze's Invasion
SET NUMBERS: 7783
YEARS: 2006

DID YOU KNOW?
Wayne Enterprises includes Wayne Technologies, Wayne Medical, Wayne Foods, Wayne Weapons, Wayne Airlines, Wayne Energy, Wayne Entertainment and more!

Classic LEGO hair, around since 1979!

Same smirk as Colonel Hardy

Sharp suit also used in LEGO® Indiana Jones™ theme

BECOMING BATMAN
A bridge in Bruce's Batcave leads to a gym and a chamber where Bruce can change into his Batsuit. But beware! It also has a trapdoor to a cage below.

Bruce is the billionaire boss of Wayne Enterprises. He raises money for charity through the Wayne Foundation, throws lavish parties and often features in Gotham City's gossip columns. (He's also secretly Batman – but don't tell anybody!)

BATMAN
THE MAN IN BLACK

VITAL STATS

LIKES: Gotham City
DISLIKES: Crime
FRIENDS: Commissioner Gordon
FOES: The Joker
SKILLS: Scaring bad guys
GEAR: Bulletproof armour, Utility Belt

SET NAMES: The Batmobile: Two-Face's Escape, The Batcave: The Penguin and Mr. Freeze's Invasion, Arkham Asylum
SET NUMBERS: 7781, 7783, 7785
YEARS: 2006

DID YOU KNOW?
An exclusive San Diego Comic-Con giveaway in 2005 included this version of Batman along with the Joker.

Pointy bat ears for a scary silhouette!

Armour moulded around muscles

BAT PACK
Batman can't fly like Superman, but when the Riddler, Scarecrow and Poison Ivy break out of Arkham Asylum (set 7785), he tracks them down using this giant bat-shaped jetpack.

Utility Belt can carry grapple gun and smoke bombs

Batman is the protector of Gotham City. When the Bat-Signal shines in the sky, he answers the call to action – sweeping in from the shadows or blasting onto the scene in his Batmobile.

BATMAN
THE CAPED CRUSADER

VITAL STATS

LIKES: Big pockets for tools
DISLIKES: Criminals running amok in Gotham City
FRIENDS: Robin
FOES: The Riddler, Bane, Scarecrow
SKILLS: Criminology
GEAR: Bat-cuffs

SET NAMES: The Batcopter: The Chase for Scarecrow, The Bat-Tank: The Riddler and Bane's Hideout
SET NUMBERS: 7786, 7787
YEARS: 2007

DID YOU KNOW?

There have been at least 30 different bat-symbols since Batman's comic-book debut in 1940.

Blue cowl looks good in the moonlight!

Simple bat-symbol

Chunky Utility Belt

2007

Lead-lined cowl

Arched bat-symbol

Five-pointed cape echoes bat-symbol

VITAL STATS

LIKES: Not being seen
DISLIKES: Smiling for photos
FRIENDS: Alfred
FOES: The Joker, Catwoman, Killer Croc
SKILLS: Nighttime camouflage
GEAR: Batwing launcher

SET NAMES: The Batman Dragster: Catwoman Pursuit, The Batboat: Hunt for Killer Croc, The Batwing: The Joker's Aerial Assault
SET NUMBERS: 7779, 7780, 7782
YEARS: 2006

2006

LIKES: Dark nights
DISLIKES: Bright colours
FRIENDS: Commissioner Gordon
FOES: The Joker, Harley Quinn, Mr. Freeze
SKILLS: Extreme physical endurance
GEAR: Batarangs

SET NAMES: Batman's Buggy: The Escape of Mr. Freeze, The Batcycle: Harley Quinn's Hammer Truck, The Tumbler: Joker's Ice Cream Surprise
SET NUMBERS: 7884, 7886, 7888
YEARS: 2008

Listening device in right ear of cowl

Flexible kevlar armour

2008

Utility Belt includes Tumbler remote control

COMIC CHARACTER

At the San Diego Comic-Con in 2011 this exclusive Batman minifigure was released to mark the relaunch of the LEGO® DC Comics Super Heroes range. His armour is darker and tougher.

DID YOU KNOW?
All Batman minifigures released before 2011 have the same face printing, with serious eyes, a stern mouth and a white sweatband.

The Caped Crusader dresses to impress, updating his outfits as crime fighting fashion dictates. Blue, black and grey are his go-to colours, with a belt to add a bit of bling. But while the details may change, the iconic cape and cowl mean he's always unmistakably Batman!

BATMOBILE
BACK IN TOWN

VITAL STATS

OWNER: Batman
USED FOR: Catching crooks
GEAR: Mega-missile

SET NAME: The Batmobile:
Two-Face's Escape
SET NUMBER: 7781
YEAR: 2006

Flexible fins
shaped like
bats' wings

Power flows to
all four wheels
via chunky pipes

Lever
launches
missile

Rubber-nosed
missile

Headlights are
stickers

BATMAN'S BUGGY

The Caped Crusader pursues
another crook in Batman's Buggy:
The Escape of Mr Freeze (set
7884). His Buggy is smaller than
the Batmobile, but still stops
traffic with its built-in gadgets.

This version of the Batmobile
packs a real punch, with a huge
missile loaded between the front
wheels. When Batman uses this
surprise weapon against Two-
Face, it blasts the villain right off
the roof of his getaway truck!

BATMAN DRAGSTER
FOR GOING ON A LONG DRIVE

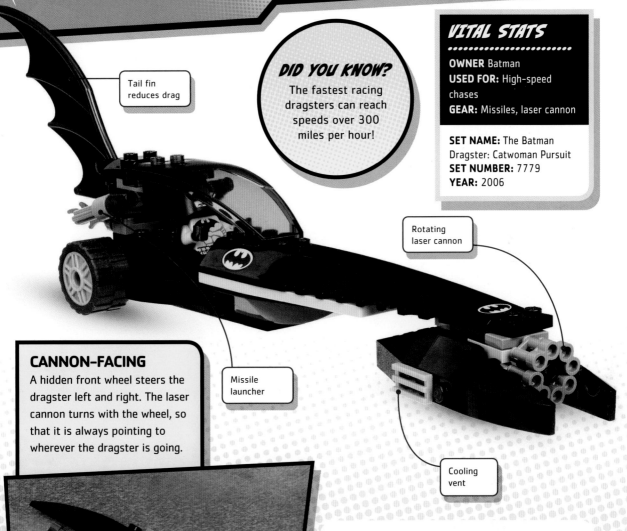

Tail fin reduces drag

DID YOU KNOW?
The fastest racing dragsters can reach speeds over 300 miles per hour!

VITAL STATS
••••••••••••••••••••
OWNER Batman
USED FOR: High-speed chases
GEAR: Missiles, laser cannon

SET NAME: The Batman Dragster: Catwoman Pursuit
SET NUMBER: 7779
YEAR: 2006

Rotating laser cannon

CANNON-FACING
A hidden front wheel steers the dragster left and right. The laser cannon turns with the wheel, so that it is always pointing to wherever the dragster is going.

Missile launcher

Cooling vent

Batman built this dragster for speed. Where wider vehicles are slowed by the wind, this dart-like design can slice through Gotham City's streets like a scythe. Its shape and speed also make it a hard target to hit in a battle.

THE BATBOAT
BAT ON THE WATER

Bat-shaped wings
leave no doubt who
owns this craft!

Twin propellers
are linked and
turn together

Space to store jet
ski behind cockpit

CRAFTY GETAWAY

A one-person jet ski fits into
the back of the Batboat. Small
enough to speed along narrow
rivers or even sewers, it's the
perfect craft to pursue Killer
Croc's speedboat.

This heavily armed hovercraft
is ideal for chasing Killer Croc.
Like all hovercraft, it can skim over
water or land on a cushion of air,
and is powered by large propellers.
Unlike other hovercraft, it also has
a pair of cool bat-shaped wings!

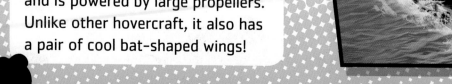

BATWING
A SYMBOL OF HOPE

VITAL STATS
....

OWNER: Batman
USED FOR: Aerial battles
GEAR: Missile launcher, rockets

SET NAME: The Batwing: The Joker's Aerial Assault
SET NUMBER: 7782
YEAR: 2006

Missile launcher folds away into tail

Missile in flight

Back wings lift to reveal rockets

Forward prongs can snare enemies in mid-air

LANDING GEAR
The Batwing has its own landing bay in the Batcave, with a folding ladder that leads to the cockpit. It is always ready for vertical take-off, straight up into the sky.

If Gotham City comes under attack from the air, Batman takes to the skies in this special fighter jet. It is shaped like the bat-symbol, so that the citizens below can look up and see that the Caped Crusader is on the case.

BATCOPTER
FLYING WITHOUT WINGS

VITAL STATS

OWNER: Batman
USED FOR: Patrolling the skies
GEAR: Lasers, rockets, missile

SET NAME: The Batcopter: The Chase for Scarecrow
SET NUMBER: 7786
YEAR: 2007

Rotor blades fold up when not in use

Targeting display

Air-to-air missile

Jet fuel goes in here

Twin laser cannons

CROW VS. BAT
When Batman battles the Scarecrow, he needs a biplane-busting missile to stop the raggedy wrongdoer from dropping fear-gas bombs on the people below!

Like the Batwing, this high-tech helicopter can take off and land vertically, without the need for a runway. It can also hover in one place in mid-air, making it useful for Batman's escapes and rescue missions.

BAT-TANK
CAN'T BE STOPPED IN ITS TRACKS!

Batman is well protected lying down inside the Bat-Tank

DID YOU KNOW?
Batman has more than 10 different Batmobiles, but only one Bat-Tank!

Triple missile launcher comes with yellow side missiles and a rubber-nosed rocket.

ENTER THROUGH GATE
The bunker-busting Bat-Tank has no problem breaking in to Bane's fortified hideout, easily knocking down the chained-up gates that come with this set.

Caterpillar tracks turn on inner wheels

What's a Super Hero to do when he already owns cars, motorcycles, boats, planes and helicopters? Get a tank, of course! Batman's Bat-Tank has huge tracks for crawling over tough terrain and a weapons turret with two types of missile.

THE TUMBLER
READY TO RUMBLE

Rear missiles hide beneath the Tumbler's sharp angles.

DID YOU KNOW?
The Tumbler was originally designed to leap across rivers and deploy bridges linking one side to the other.

Raised fins assist braking

Smaller front wheels for tight turns

SECRET WEAPON
The back of the Tumbler has a hidden launcher that flips up to fire a large rubber-tipped missile. The missile can be locked in place with a LEGO® Technic pin.

Twin machine guns lie between the front wheels

This angular assault vehicle is heavily armed with two different types of missile. The cockpit has room for Batman and a passenger (or a handcuffed prisoner!), and four extra-large back wheels power the vehicle into battle.

BATMAN
CLASSIC-STYLE CAPED CRUSADER

VITAL STATS

LIKES: Rescue missions
DISLIKES: Terrible traps
FRIENDS: Robin
FOES: The Joker, the Riddler, Harley Quinn
SKILLS: Motorcycle stunts
GEAR: Batarangs, Batmobile

SET NAMES: The Dynamic Duo Funhouse Escape, The Batcave
SET NUMBERS: 6857, 6860
YEARS: 2012

Batman's eyes cannot be seen through his suit's cowl.

Fabric cloak for dramatic poses

Batman's trusty Batarang has appeared in more than 20 LEGO sets.

Classic bat-symbol on a bright yellow disk

Gadgets can be attached to Utility Belt.

SPREADING HIS WINGS

To stop Catwoman from making a purr-fect getaway, Batman swaps his cape for glider wings and a jetpack to take to the air and chase after her in Catwoman Catcycle City Chase (set 6858).

Heroic Batman dons this classic comic book colour scheme to free Robin from a fiendish funfair. His blue and grey suit is more than enough to strike terror into Gotham's super-villain community.

BRUCE WAYNE
CRIME-FIGHTING BILLIONAIRE

VITAL STATS

LIKES: The Batcave
DISLIKES: Drill tanks
FRIENDS: Robin
FOES: Poison Ivy, Bane
SKILLS: A quick Bat-change
GEAR: Bat-phone

SET NAME: The Batcave
SET NUMBER: 6860
YEAR: 2012

DID YOU KNOW?
Bruce's stern expression is similar to the face you'll find under the Batman minifigure's cowl.

Slicked-back black hair

Chiselled cheekbones and a serious expression

A stylish sand-blue suit

THE CALL TO ACTION
Bruce knows about trouble as soon as the phone rings. Luckily, the lift is ready to transform him into Batman and drop him into the fight!

BAT-GEAR

Billionaire Bruce Wayne puts his vast riches to good use fighting crime as Batman, and yet his worst nightmare comes true when Bane drills into the top-secret Batcave. Bruce doesn't want anyone to discover his secret identity.

BATMAN
ELECTRO SUIT SHOCKER

VITAL STATS

LIKES: Gotham City
DISLIKES: Law-breaking
FRIENDS: Robin
FOES: Gotham City's criminal community
SKILLS: Delivering electric shocks
GEAR: Electro suit

SET NAME: DK's LEGO DC Universe™ Super Heroes Batman™ Visual Dictionary Exclusive
SET NUMBER: N/A
YEAR: 2012

DID YOU KNOW?

The Electro suit made its first appearance in the LEGO Batman 2: DC Super Heroes video game.

No oval for the bat-symbol

A double-sided head also includes a smiling face on the other side.

POWER POINTS

Without a cape, the taser points on the back of Batman's minifigure are clearly visible. Bruce designed the suit to release charges from both the front and rear. What a clever spark!

Light blue lines show where electricity can be generated.

Taser points

Sometimes even Batman's martial arts aren't enough to bring down Gotham City's super-villains. The Dark Knight's Electro suit amps up the action by delivering an electric shock with every punch.

BATWING
FLIGHT AND FIGHT

VITAL STATS

OWNER: Batman
USED FOR: Flying like a bat
GEAR: Homing missile, rocket launchers

SET NAMES: Batwing Battle Over Gotham City
SET NUMBERS: 6863
YEARS: 2012

Rear wings can tilt up and down

Tail covers flaming exhaust

Front lights for night flying

Wings echo Bat-symbol shape

BACK BUTTON
Flipping up the cover behind the cockpit reveals a hidden button. Pressing it launches a homing missile that has Batarang-like wings, which is docked on the underside of the vessel.

DID YOU KNOW?
The world's biggest bats can have wingspans of up to 170cm (5ft 6in).

Batman is ready to take on airborne enemies in his custom-built Batwing. It has rocket launchers hidden beneath its back wings and a homing missile under its tail, and is shaped like a bat so his opponents know who is coming for them!

BATMOBILE
GOOD LOOKS CATCH CROOKS!

VITAL STATS

OWNER: Batman
USED FOR: Fighting crime, looking cool
GEAR: Missiles

SET NAMES: Batmobile and the Two-Face Chase
SET NUMBERS: 6864
YEARS: 2012

Batwings protect rear engine from side-on attacks

Twin missile launchers

Cooling stacks

Plush red interior has room for Batman in his cape

Vents draw air into engine at rear

ARMS RACE
The Batmobile takes on a crane truck full of crooks when Two-Face and his henchmen raid a bank. Both cars fire super-fast missiles, but whose will hit their target first?

The sleek curves of the Batmobile hug the ground for a literal low profile – but the bright yellow wheels and flaming exhaust make for a pretty high-profile warning to crooks. Just one glimpse makes some of them quit crime altogether!

ARCTIC BATBOAT
IN POLE POSITION

VITAL STATS
....

OWNER: Batman
USED FOR: Sledding over ice
GEAR: Disc launchers,
ice bombs

SET NAMES: Arctic Batman
vs. Mr Freeze : Aquaman
on Ice
SET NUMBERS: 76000
YEARS: 2013

Batwing rudder
assists steering

BACK WITH A BANG
As well as fast-flying discs
launched from the front of
the vessel, the Arctic Batboat is
also armed with a pair of
ice-busting bombs at the back.

Targeting
computer display

Blades for skiing
over ice and
snow

Batman brings the heat in his
Arctic Batboat! Designed to
withstand the coldest conditions, it
cuts across ice and snow at speed.
That makes it the perfect rescue
craft when Aquaman gets frozen in
a block of ice by Mr Freeze.

ARCTIC BATMAN
A COLD KNIGHT

This minifigure uses the second version of Batman's LEGO cowl.

Bat-symbol in white and grey

White polar batsuit blends in with the snow

A COLD SENSE OF HUMOUR

Batman isn't always the warmest character, but a twist of the hero's head reveals a less frosty side. Even in icy conditions, the Dark Knight keeps his cool.

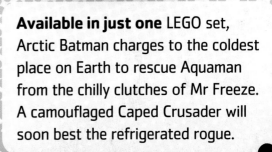

Available in just one LEGO set, Arctic Batman charges to the coldest place on Earth to rescue Aquaman from the chilly clutches of Mr Freeze. A camouflaged Caped Crusader will soon best the refrigerated rogue.

BATMAN
THE BANE OF BANE

Black cowl covers double-sided head

Sharp-edged bat-symbol

Printed body armour

Complex bronze Utility Belt

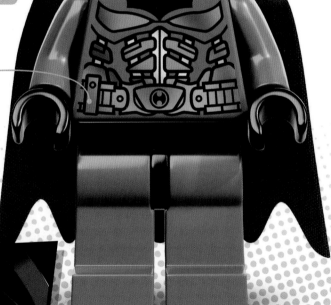

SAFE AND SOUND
Bane safely dispatched, Batman gives Gordon a lift back to police HQ in the Bat. Thanks to his alternate face, the Dark Knight looks happy to help out his old friend.

When this armoured Batman spots Bane chasing down Commissioner Gordon in a stolen Tumbler, he swoops to the rescue in the Bat. This set is inspired by the 2012 *The Dark Knight Rises* movie.

SCUBA BATMAN
DEEP-SEA DETECTIVE

VITAL STATS

LIKES: Diving
DISLIKES: Jewel thieves
FRIENDS: Commissioner Gordon
FOES: The Penguin
SKILLS: First-class swimmer
GEAR: Scuba gear, harpoon

SET NAMES: Batman: The Penguin Face Off
SET NUMBERS: 76010
YEARS: 2014

Dark blue cowl accompanied by a scowl

Harpoon gun at the ready

Breathing apparatus leading to air tanks worn on the back

Flippers for fast swimming action

TAKE A DEEP BREATH
Scuba Batman's alternate face sees the Dark Knight wearing his breathing apparatus. The Penguin will be in hot water when Batman reels him in for stealing Gotham City's gems.

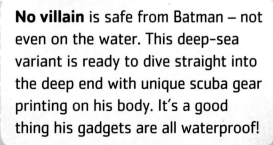

No villain is safe from Batman – not even on the water. This deep-sea variant is ready to dive straight into the deep end with unique scuba gear printing on his body. It's a good thing his gadgets are all waterproof!

SCUBA VEHICLE
CHARTING NEW DEPTHS

VITAL STATS

OWNER: Batman
USED FOR: Diving
GEAR: Torpedo launchers

SET NAME: Batman: The Penguin Face Off
SET NUMBER: 76010
YEAR: 2014

Batman in scuba gear

Harpoon gun

Clips to hold harpoon

Torpedo in flight

Fins steer left and right

TWO BIRDS, ONE STONE

Batman uses his Scuba Vehicle to find a stolen diamond that is guarded by two of the Penguin's robot helpers.

This solo speeder dives down underwater so Batman can face his fishiest foes. It is small enough not to show up on enemy sensors, but is still effective, thanks to its twin torpedoes, powerful engine and fishlike fins for steering.

BATCOPTER
A WHOLE NEW SPIN

VITAL STATS

OWNER: Batman
USED FOR: Pest control
GEAR: Missiles, winch

SET NAME: Batman: The Riddler Chase
SET NUMBER: 76012
YEAR: 2014

Jet engines on both sides

Missile in launcher

Batwing-shaped tail fin

Missile in flight

HOOKED!
Turning a gear at the back of the Batcopter lowers a hook on a rope. Turning the gear the other way reels in whatever – or whoever – the winch has hooked.

Flybars add stability

Winch can snare villains or rescue friends

There's only room for one Bat over Gotham City! So when the monstrous Man-Bat launches an aerial attack, Batman breaks out his brilliant Batcopter. If its weapons don't clip Man-Bat's wings, its winch will bring him down to earth!

Project Editor Emma Grange
Editors Tina Jindal, Pamela Afram, Matt Jones,
Clare Millar, Ellie Barton, Rosie Peet
Senior Designers Nathan Martin, Mark Penfound,
David McDonald
Designers Karan Chaudhary, Stefan Georgiou
Pre-Production Producer Siu Yin Chan
Senior Producer Lloyd Robertson
Managing Editors Paula Regan,
Chitra Subramanyam
Design Managers Neha Ahuja, Guy Harvey
Creative Manager Sarah Harland
Art Director Lisa Lanzarini
Publisher Julie Ferris
Publishing Director Simon Beecroft

Additional Photography Markos Chouris,
Christopher Chouris, Gary Ombler

First published in Great Britain in 2016
by Dorling Kindersley Limited
80 Strand, London, WC2R ORL

001–298875–Jul/16

Contains content previously published in LEGO® DC COMICS
SUPER HEROES *Character Encyclopedia* (2016)

Page design copyright © 2016 Dorling Kindersley Limited
A Penguin Random House Company

A CIP catalogue record for this book
is available from the British Library.

ISBN: 978-0-2412-9283-9

Printed and bound in China

www.LEGO.com
www.dk.com
A WORLD OF IDEAS:
SEE ALL THERE IS TO KNOW

ACKNOWLEDGEMENTS

DK would like to thank Randi Sørensen,
Paul Hansford, Martin Leighton Lindhardt, Maria
Bloksgaard Markussen, Adam Corbally, Daniel
Mckenna, Casper Glahder, Adam Siegmund Grabowski,
John Cuppage, Justin Ramsden, Karl Oskar Jonas
Norlen, Marcos Bessa, Sally Aston, Sven Robin Kahl
and Mauricio Bedolla at the LEGO Group; Ben Harper,
Thomas Zellers and Melanie Swartz at Warner Bros.;
Cavan Scott and Simon Hugo for their writing;
Katie Bowden for editorial assistance and Sam
Bartlett for design assistance.